The Whooping Crane

by
Bonnie Graves

Perfection Learning®

Cover Photo: Courtesy of the International Crane Foundation
Inside Illustration: James Needham: pp 8, 10, 11, 35.
Randy Messer: pp 7, 15, 33.

Dedication

To my dear family, nature lovers all, especially Mike, Esther, Diann, and Jake, who all give their special brand of tender loving care to the creatures of the air . . . and to Margo, who gave this story wings.

Acknowledgments

I would like to thank Debbie Carley, Publicity Coordinator at the International Crane Foundation in Baraboo, Wisconsin, for introducing me to Gee Whiz and his "lady" friend, Oobleck, and also for tracking down answers to my many questions. I am also grateful to Marianne Wellington, lead aviculturalist at the International Crane Foundation, for her valuable input on the story; to my mother, Helen Beecher, for helping with research, story ideas, and getting Gee Whiz to show off for us; and to James Lewis, National Whooping Crane Coordinator at the U.S. Fish and Wildlife Service, for reading and commenting on the manuscript.

Special acknowledgment is also due to my uncle, Jacob Valentine, Junior, whose lifelong work with cranes provided the inspiration for this project; to Dr. Ray Erickson, who actually flew with the baby whooper, Tex, and to Barbara Katz who wrote about it; and to all those individuals who give their time, talents, and resources to preserving this magnificent species.

About the Author

Bonnie Graves is the author of *The Best Worst Day* and *Mystery of the Tooth Gremlin*—two chapter books for beginning readers. A third, *How Do You Spell Gabrielle?*, is soon to be published.

Mrs. Graves has also written for the television science show *Newton's Apple* and with her husband, Michael, coauthored a number of books and articles on reading. Before she began her career as a writer, she taught elementary school in California.

Now Mrs. Graves and her husband live in Bloomington, Minnesota, at the edge of a huge park reserve. The reserve is home to deer, fox, raccoons, muskrats, owls, pheasants, and a number of migratory and nonmigratory birds. They have two daughters, Julie and Erin, and a cat named Sunshine. The whole family loves the out-of-doors—to hike, cross-country ski, and explore the wonders of nature, especially in their own backyard.

US Fish & Wildlife

Contents

Chapter 1

Trouble Aboard
Flight #56

<u>Dallas, Texas, 1967</u>

"Tex could die without my care," the man told the airline captain. "Don't you understand?"

"I do understand, sir. And I'm sorry. But rules are rules," the captain said. "No animals where food is served."

Megan listened to the men. Their stern voices made her uneasy.

Megan looked up at the captain. She looked at the man sitting next to her. Then she looked at the cardboard box on his lap.

Megan heard a peep from inside the box. What sort of animal was in there?

The captain took the box from the man. "Tex will be fine with the bags, Doctor. Don't worry."

Megan read the look on the doctor's face. He was worried! A lot. He stood up and watched the captain walk away with the box.

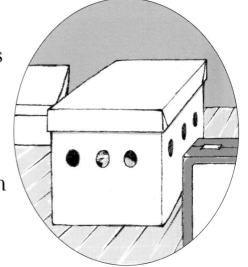

The man fell back into his seat. "How can he do this?"

Suddenly he glanced at Megan. He looked surprised to see her sitting there.

"Sorry," he said. "I forgot you were sitting there. Is this your first plane trip?"

Megan shook her head. "My dad lives in Maryland. I've visited him every summer since I was six. I'm ten now."

The doctor nodded. "I'm going to Maryland too. With Tex. If Tex makes it."

2

Endangered Species

"What kind of animal is Tex?" Megan asked.

"A whooping crane. A chick just 16 days old. An **endangered species.** Do you know what that is?" asked the man.

Megan said, "It means there aren't too many whooping cranes left. And they might become **extinct.** Like the dinosaurs."

"Right!" said the doctor. "Very smart. What's your name?"

"Megan Blake," answered the girl. "Are you an animal doctor?"

"Glad to meet you, Megan. Well, I am a doctor. But I don't take care of people. I'm a **biologist.** I study animals. I care what happens to them. That's why I'm taking care of the crane." The doctor stuck out his hand. Megan shook it.

"Tex hatched two weeks ago at the San Antonio Zoo. I'm taking her to the Patuxent Wildlife Research Center," he told Megan.

ICF Photo

"What's that?" she asked.

"A place where endangered birds get special care. The best care possible," answered the doctor.

He continued, "If Tex makes it to be an adult, that will mean one more whooper.

14

"There are only 55 living now. I know, 55 doesn't sound like a lot.

"Some scientists think that before the settlers came, there were 5,000 whoopers in North America. By the middle 1800s, there were only 500 to 800 cranes left. In 1941, only 15 whoopers were alive."

The plane started down the runway.

"Then Tex is number 56," Megan said.

"What's that?" the doctor asked over the engine noise.

"Tex is whooping crane number 56," Megan said louder.

Megan felt the speeding plane shake. Her back pressed against the seat. The plane lifted off the ground.

She thought of the baby whooper riding in a box all by herself with the bags. "Whooping crane number 56. If she lives," Megan thought.

Chapter 3

What Happened?

"What happened to the whoopers? Why are there so few left?" Megan asked.

"People shot them. Collected their eggs," the doctor said.

"But worst of all, people destroyed their nesting places. The **wetlands** were drained. And the grasslands became farms.

"Twice a year, whoopers fly 2,500 miles," the doctor continued. "That's more than twice as far as you and I will fly today. Along the way, they need places to land. Places with food and water. Wetlands."

Undisturbed wetlands

ICF Photo

Wetlands being destroyed

ICF Photo

Megan looked out the window. The plane was high above the ground.

What if she were a bird and people were shooting at her? With all those houses and highways, where would she find food and water? Megan wondered how many wetlands were left for the birds.

"Want to see the whooping cranes' **migratory path?**" the doctor asked.

"Sure," answered Megan.

The man opened the flight magazine to a map. He pointed to it. "The birds winter here in Aransas National Wildlife Refuge in Texas. Then they **migrate** north around late March or early April.

ICF Photo

18

"They fly over many states on their way to Canada. Once in Canada, they fly to Wood Buffalo National Park. They arrive at these nesting grounds in late April or early May," the doctor explained.

"In the fall, whoopers fly south. They leave their nesting place in Wood Buffalo National Park. Two days later, they're in the fields of southern Saskatchewan," said the doctor.

Wood Buffalo National Park in Canada   ICF Photo

The man continued. "The cranes spend two to four weeks eating grain in these fields. Then they're ready to finish their trip south.

"The whooping cranes make the trip to Texas in about 10 days. In all, it takes the cranes about 30 days to fly from Canada to Texas."

"How do they know the way?" asked Megan.

"Fledgling whoopers follow their parents," the doctor explained. "South in the fall and north in the spring."

ICF Photo

Megan tried to picture these birds in her mind. She tried to see them flying toward Canada.

ICF Photo

"I've never seen a whooping crane. What do they look like?" she asked.

"They are the most beautiful birds in the sky. And the tallest in North America. Five feet tall with a seven-foot **wingspan,**" the doctor explained.

"They have a snow-white body. And black wing tips that you can see when they fly. Here. I'll show you." He opened a

ICF Photo

folder. It held several pictures of cranes.

"What's that?" Megan asked. She pointed to the red cap on top of the crane's head.

"Red skin," the doctor answered. "Cranes use that red like a stop sign.

They bend their heads down to show it. That means *stay away!*"

Megan gazed out the window. She thought how wonderful it would be to see a whooping crane fly by!

She hoped Tex was OK. Megan tried to picture the baby whooper in her box. Tex was flying to Maryland without flapping her wings once! If she made it.

Time to Eat

The flight attendant brought lunch.

"No, thank you," the doctor said. "I'm not hungry. Too worried about Tex."

Megan, however, was starved. She was glad for her tray of food. Glad she didn't have to fly over Texas looking for it!

"What do whooping cranes eat?" she asked the doctor. She unwrapped a roll and buttered it.

"Oh, lots of different things. It depends on where they are. And what they can find," the doctor answered.

"Whoopers eat grain and insects. But they also eat acorns, berries, crabs, and clams."

He glanced at Megan. "Whooper chicks have quite an appetite too. They grow almost an inch a day. And they gain over 20 percent of their weight in a day!"

"Wow!" Megan said. "What if I grew as fast as a baby crane? Let's see. I'm 4 feet 8 inches tall and weigh 70 pounds. I'm visiting my dad for two weeks. By the time I went home, I'd be . . ."

The doctor pulled out a notepad and pencil. "You'd be 5 feet 10 inches tall! And you'd weigh 744 pounds!"

Megan's Growth Chart

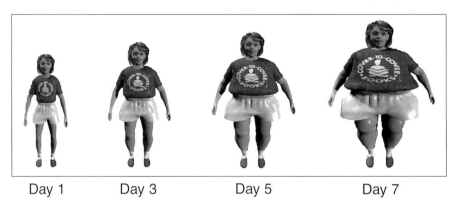

Day 1   Day 3   Day 5   Day 7

Day 9   Day 11   Day 14

At that moment Megan heard a shriek somewhere. "What was that?"

"If I didn't know better, I'd say Tex escaped," the doctor replied.

Chapter 5

Whooper Calls

The doctor looked down the aisle. "Oh, it's an unhappy baby."

"Is that really the sound a whooper makes?" Megan asked.

"Well, not exactly," the doctor answered. "When a whooper's stressed, it shrieks. The scream sounds sort of like a whine.

"If it's looking for its parents, it makes a little contact call," the doctor added. "Like a chirping cricket.

"When it's getting fed, it gives an excited, begging call. Sometimes that sounds like a purr. Other times it sounds like an excited chirp," the doctor said.

"Did you know that the whooping crane got its name because of its loud call?" he asked. "It's like a bugle call that can be heard three miles away!"

"Wow!" cried Megan. "That's how far away my best friend lives. Three miles. We clocked it on our bikes. If I could yell as loud as a whooper, I wouldn't need the telephone!"

"But you'd have to have a long neck like a whooper," explained the doctor. "They have a **trachea**, or windpipe, that's five feet long!"

"That's taller than I am!" Megan said. "Why do whoopers have such a loud call?"

"Good question!" the doctor said. "They use it to say things like 'Danger!' or 'Watch out!'

ICF Photo

29

"Or 'Stay out of this place. It belongs to my family!' " the doctor continued.

"Or 'Want to be my mate? Come fly with me!' "

Megan giggled. "But do they have to shout?"

"If you saw your friend across the mall, what would you do?" he asked.

"Shout, of course!" laughed Megan.

Megan wondered, "Is Tex calling out from her box right now? Will anyone hear her?"

US Fish & Wildlife

Chapter

Shall We Dance?

"What will you do on your visit?" the doctor asked Megan.

"Go to the zoo in Washington, D.C. And see the ballet in New York City. I want to be a dancer when I grow up," Megan said. She popped the last bite of cookie into her mouth.

"Well, then you have something else in common with whooping cranes. Besides a good appetite," he said.

Megan laughed. "They want to be dancers?"

ICF Photo

"They are dancers," the doctor said.

"No way!" cried Megan.

"Oh, yes," the doctor laughed. "Male and female whoopers dance with each other. They bow, jump up in the air, and flap their wings. It's really beautiful to see. Quite amazing."

Megan tried to picture dancing cranes. She wished she could see cranes dance.

"You mean Tex is going to dance someday?" she asked.

The man's smile turned into a frown. Megan knew he was thinking of the baby whooper riding with the bags.

Was she still alive? Would Tex have the chance to dance with another whooping crane someday?

7

Touchdown

Megan heard a voice over the loudspeaker.

"Please remain seated until the plane has come to a complete stop and the captain has turned off the seat belt sign."

Megan couldn't believe the flight was over. In just over three hours, she had traveled half as many miles as the whoopers did in 30 days.

And the cranes had to hunt for food and water along the way. The flight attendant had brought hers.

She thought about Tex with the bags. Had the baby whooper needed food and water on the three-hour flight? Did she stay warm enough? Was she still alive?

"Nice meeting you, Megan," the doctor said. "I'm going to say good-bye now. As soon as the plane stops, I'm going to race out. I have to get to the tail of the plane before they unload Tex."

A few seconds later Megan looked out the window. She saw a cardboard box bouncing down the belt with the bags!

Poor Tex! The doctor hadn't even gotten off the plane yet!

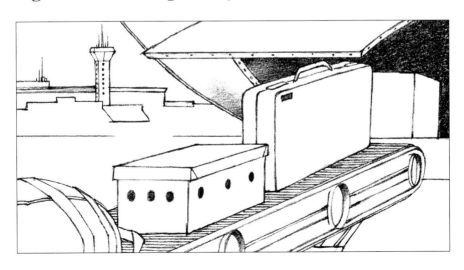

Chapter

Tex!

Megan hurried off the plane. She walked quickly to the gate area. Right away she spotted her dad.

"Dad! Hi!" cried Megan.

Megan's dad smiled and hugged her.

"Wow! Have you grown!" he said.

"I guess so. But not as much as if I were a baby whooping crane!" laughed Megan.

"What?" Megan's dad looked puzzled.

"Dad, I had the best plane ride. I rode on the same plane with an endangered species. A whooping crane and . . ."

"Megan!"

Megan turned around. The doctor was walking toward her. He held a cardboard box.

"Look!" he said to her.

Megan looked in the box. There was a fluffy bird with rust-colored feathers.

"Oh, Tex!" she said. "You made it!"

Megan looked up at the doctor and smiled. "Whooper number 56. Hooray!"

ICF Photo

37

Tex's first day at the International
Crane Foundation in Baraboo,
Wisconsin

ICF Photos

38

Epilogue

Thirty years later, 1997

The story of Tex really happened.

In 1967, Dr. Ray Erickson, a biologist, was taking 16-day-old Tex to Patuxent Wildlife Research Center in Laurel, Maryland. He boarded a plane in Dallas, Texas. He was told that Tex would have to fly with the bags.

Tex lived through the trip. And for the next several years, she lived at Patuxent Wildlife Center in Maryland.

In 1976, Tex was sent to the International Crane Foundation in Baraboo, Wisconsin. And with the help of the director, George Archibald, her one and only **offspring,** Gee Whiz, was hatched. After Tex had laid the egg, it was placed in an **incubator.** The egg was cared for by people until it hatched.

Gee Whiz at the International Crane Foundation in Baraboo, Wisconsin

Just 21 days after the egg hatched, Tex was killed by raccoons that broke into her pen.

However, Gee Whiz is still alive and well in Baraboo. You can see him there. He likes to show off for visitors.

Today if a crane chick had to take an airplane ride, its journey would be much different from Tex's flight in 1967.

A chick would have its own seat next to its keeper. It would ride in a special crate with air holes.

A tape recording of a **brood call** would be next to the crate. That's the sound a whooping crane's parents make when they hold their chick under their wings to keep it warm.

The chick's keeper would also have food. The keeper would carry crane chick chow and treats of mealworms, earthworms, and pinkies (baby mice).

A puppet would be used to feed the baby. The keeper would reach into the crate with a crane-head puppet holding the food.

Baby cranes need to imprint with their own kind. *Imprinting* means identifying with whoever acts as a parent to them.

Scientists learned about imprinting the hard way. Because humans raised and cared for Tex, she thought she was a human. Not a whooping crane. When it came time to mate, she would have nothing to do with male cranes.

Now crane keepers wear crane costumes with a puppet head to help young cranes imprint as a crane.

ICF Photo

Over the past 30 years, people who love cranes have done a great deal to help this endangered species grow in numbers. As of 1996, there were a total of 356 whooping cranes.

But this rare and beautiful bird is still in danger of extinction. To find out more about whooping cranes and how you can help, write to the address below.

The International Crane Foundation
P.O. Box 447
Baraboo, WI 53913

44

Whooping Crane Facts

height	up to 5½ feet tall; the tallest bird in North America
weight	male—16 pounds; female—14 pounds
wingspan	7–8 feet
color	pure white with black wing tips, black legs and feet, black facial markings, and a bare patch of red skin on the head
features	unwebbed feet; 5-foot-long trachea; a bugle call that can be heard up to 3 miles

Photo: Bonnie Graves

family life Cranes pair for life at about 4 or 5 years old. Crane couples dance before they mate. Generally, the female lays two eggs a season. Rarely three. Males and females take turns sitting on the eggs to hatch them. Only one usually lives to fledgling age.

ICF Photo

46

habitat and home	North American wetlands. On summer nesting grounds, each pair claims a territory of about 300 acres. They protect this area from other whoopers and enemies. Nests are built on a 3-foot-tall mound of plants in shallow ponds. Pairs return to the same nesting sites year after year.
food	grain, insects, acorns, berries, crabs, and clams
enemies	Raccoons, bobcats, power lines, and disease. Drought is also a threat. Nesting areas are exposed to **predators.** And food is hard to find. Cranes' major threat to survival is the disappearing wetlands.
life span	25 years

where found

In the wild, whooping cranes can be found along two migratory routes. One is from Wood Buffalo National Park in Canada to Aransas National Wildlife Refuge in Texas. The other is from Grays Lake, Idaho, to Bosque del Apache, New Mexico. Florida is the home of a **nonmigratory** flock of whoopers.

Nonmigratory flock in Florida   ICF Photo

population   In August 1996 there were a total of 356 whooping cranes in the wild and captivity.

cousins   There are 15 species of crane all over the world. Counting the whooping crane, seven of these species are endangered.

A Whooping Crane
Photo Gallery

Photos: US Fish & Wildlife

Photos: US Fish & Wildlife

Glossary

biologist   scientist who studies plant and animal life

brood call   sound an animal makes to its young

endangered species   species in danger of extinction

extinct   no longer existing or living

fledgling   young bird that has just learned to fly

ICF Photo

imprinting	rapid learning process that takes place early in life that causes an animal to recognize and be attracted to its own kind
incubator	a device in which eggs are hatched artificially
migrate	to move from one place or climate to another for feeding or nesting
migratory path	route used to move from place to place
nonmigratory	stays in one place or climate
offspring	young of a plant or animal
predator	animal that hunts another

trachea   tube through which air passes to and from the lungs; windpipe

wetlands   land areas containing much soil moisture; swamps

wingspan   the distance between wing tips